TABLE OF C(

HOW TO USE A FOUNTAIN PEN

Exploring Calligraphy, Lettering, & Artistic Expression

James Roland

Chapter 1

The World of Fountain Pens: A Deep Dive into History, Types, Anatomy, and How They Work

Welcome to the captivating world of fountain pens! In this chapter, we'll embark on a journey through time to explore the fascinating history of these writing instruments. We'll delve into the diverse array of fountain pens available, uncover their intricate anatomy, and understand the mechanics behind their magical ink flow. By the end of this chapter, you'll be equipped with the knowledge to choose the perfect fountain pen to accompany you on your creative adventures.

1.1 The History of Fountain Pens: A Journey Through Time

The story of fountain pens is a testament to human ingenuity and the desire for effortless and elegant writing. The concept of a self-contained reservoir pen dates back to the 10th century, but it wasn't until the 19th century that the fountain pen as we know it today began to take shape.

Early fountain pens were often messy and unreliable, with ink leaks and inconsistent flow being common problems. However, innovators and inventors like Lewis Waterman, who introduced the first commercially successful fountain pen in the 1880s, paved the way for significant improvements in design and functionality.

The 20th century saw a boom in fountain pen popularity, with various manufacturers creating unique and luxurious models. Brands like Montblanc, Parker, and Sheaffer became synonymous with quality and craftsmanship, and fountain pens became a symbol of status and sophistication.

Today, fountain pens continue to be cherished by writers, artists, and enthusiasts worldwide. Their appeal lies not only in their smooth and expressive writing experience but also in their rich history and cultural significance.

1.2 Types of Fountain Pens: Exploring the Variety

Fountain pens come in a dazzling array of styles, sizes, and materials, each with its own unique charm and characteristics. Let's take a closer look at some of the most common types:

- **Cartridge/Converter Pens:** These pens offer the convenience of pre-filled ink cartridges or the flexibility of refillable converters, making them a popular choice for beginners and those who prefer a fuss-free experience.
- **Piston-Fill Pens:** Piston-fill pens feature a built-in mechanism that allows you to draw ink directly from a bottle. They often boast a larger ink capacity than cartridge/converter

pens and are favored by those who appreciate a classic and elegant design.

- **Vacuum-Fill Pens:** These pens use a vacuum mechanism to fill the ink reservoir, offering a quick and efficient filling process. They are known for their reliability and are often sought after by collectors and enthusiasts.
- **Lever-Fill Pens:** Lever-fill pens feature a lever on the side of the barrel that, when lifted and lowered, activates a mechanism to fill the pen with ink. They are valued for their vintage aesthetic and mechanical ingenuity.
- **Eyedropper Pens:** These pens are filled by directly inserting a dropper into the barrel and filling it with ink. They are known for their simplicity and large ink capacity, but they require a bit more care and attention to avoid leaks.

In addition to these basic types, fountain pens can also be classified by their nib size (ranging from extra-fine to broad), material (ranging from resin and plastic to metal and precious metals), and even their historical significance (vintage pens from renowned manufacturers).

1.3 Anatomy of a Fountain Pen: Understanding the Components

To fully appreciate the beauty and functionality of a fountain pen, it's essential to understand its intricate components. Let's take a closer look at the anatomy of a typical fountain pen:

- **Nib:** The nib is the metal tip of the pen that comes into contact with the paper. It is responsible for delivering the ink and shaping the line you create. Nibs come in various sizes and styles, each with its own unique writing characteristics.
- **Feed:** The feed is the black plastic component located beneath the nib. It regulates the flow of ink from the reservoir to the nib, ensuring a smooth and consistent writing experience.
- **Grip Section:** The grip section is the part of the pen that you hold while writing. It is often made of a comfortable material like resin or metal and can feature ergonomic contours for a more pleasant writing experience.
- **Barrel:** The barrel is the main body of the pen that houses the ink reservoir. It can be made of various materials and often features decorative elements like engravings or patterns.
- **Cap:** The cap protects the nib when the pen is not in use and can also be posted on the back of the pen while writing for added balance and comfort.
- **Ink Reservoir:** The ink reservoir is the chamber inside the pen that holds the ink. It can be a cartridge, converter, or a built-in mechanism depending on the filling system of the pen.
- **Filling Mechanism:** The filling mechanism varies depending on the type of fountain pen and can range from cartridges and converters to piston-fillers and vacuum-fillers.

Understanding the anatomy of a fountain pen will not only deepen your appreciation for its design and craftsmanship but also make it easier to troubleshoot any issues that may arise.

1.4 How Fountain Pens Work: The Science of Ink Flow

The magic of a fountain pen lies in its ability to deliver ink smoothly and consistently to the paper. This is achieved through a combination of capillary action and gravity.

Capillary action is the tendency of a liquid to flow in narrow spaces against the force of gravity. In a fountain pen, capillary action draws ink from the reservoir, through the feed, and onto the nib. The feed is designed with channels and fins that create narrow spaces for the ink to flow, ensuring a controlled and steady supply.

Gravity also plays a role in ink flow, especially when the pen is held at an angle. The ink flows down the feed and onto the nib due to the force of gravity, aided by the capillary action.

The nib itself is a key component in ink flow. It is designed with a slit that allows ink to flow from the feed onto the paper. The width of the slit and the shape of the nib determine the line width and writing characteristics of the pen.

1.5 Choosing Your First Fountain Pen: A Guide to Finding Your Perfect Match

With so many fountain pen options available, choosing your first pen can be a daunting task. However, by considering your individual needs and preferences, you can find the perfect pen to start your journey into the world of fountain pens.

Here are some key factors to consider when choosing your first fountain pen:

- **Budget:** Fountain pens can range in price from affordable to luxurious. Set a budget that you're comfortable with and explore the options within that range.
- **Nib Size:** The nib size determines the width of the line your pen will produce. Choose a size that suits your handwriting style and preferences. Extra-fine nibs are ideal for small handwriting or detailed work, while broader nibs are great for expressive writing or calligraphy.
- **Filling Mechanism:** Consider whether you prefer the convenience of cartridges, the flexibility of converters, or the classic appeal of piston-fillers or vacuum-fillers.
- **Material & Design:** Fountain pens come in various materials like resin, metal, and precious metals. Choose a material and design that you find visually appealing and comfortable to hold.
- **Brand & Reputation:** Consider brands known for their quality and craftsmanship. While

some brands are more expensive, they often offer better warranties and customer service.

- **Try Before You Buy:** If possible, try out different pens in a store or borrow them from friends to get a feel for how they write and handle.

Remember, choosing a fountain pen is a personal journey. Take your time, explore the options, and trust your instincts to find the pen that speaks to you. Whether it's a sleek and modern design or a vintage classic, the perfect fountain pen is out there waiting to be discovered.

Chapter 2

Ink and Paper: The Essential Duo

In this chapter, we delve into the enchanting world of ink and paper – the lifeblood and canvas of the fountain pen experience. These two elements are not mere tools but partners in your artistic journey. Understanding their nuances and how they interact will unlock a world of creative possibilities. We'll explore the various types of fountain pen inks, their unique properties, and how to choose the perfect ink for your writing or artistic endeavors. We'll guide you through the intricacies of filling your pen, regardless of its mechanism, and introduce you to the vast array of papers that complement fountain pen ink beautifully. Finally, we'll delve into the art of ink and paper pairing, allowing you to create stunning visual and tactile experiences with every stroke of your pen.

2.1 Types of Fountain Pen Ink: Properties and Characteristics

Fountain pen inks are far more diverse than you might imagine. They come in a spectrum of colors, from vibrant hues to subtle shades, and offer a range of properties that affect how they behave on paper.

- **Dye-based Inks:** These inks are known for their vibrant colors and excellent flow properties. They dry quickly and are generally less prone to clogging or staining. However, they may not be as lightfast as pigmented inks, meaning their colors may fade over time when exposed to sunlight.

- **Pigmented Inks:** Pigmented inks are prized for their archival quality and exceptional lightfastness. They resist fading even when exposed to sunlight for extended periods. However, they can be more prone to clogging and may require more frequent cleaning of your pen.
- **Iron Gall Inks:** Iron gall inks have a rich history and were widely used in the past. They offer excellent water resistance and archival properties, but they can be acidic and may damage certain types of paper or pen parts over time. Modern formulations are less acidic and safer for use.
- **Shimmering Inks:** Shimmering inks contain metallic particles that add a touch of sparkle and dimension to your writing. They are available in a variety of colors and can create stunning visual effects.
- **Scented Inks:** Scented inks offer a delightful sensory experience, with subtle fragrances that complement your writing. However, some people may be sensitive to the scents, so use them with caution.

Understanding the different types of inks and their properties will help you choose the right ink for your specific needs and preferences. Whether you prioritize vibrant colors, archival quality, or unique effects, there's a fountain pen ink out there for you.

2.2 Choosing the Right Ink for Your Pen & Purpose

Selecting the right ink involves considering both your pen and your intended use. Certain inks may work better with specific pen types or filling mechanisms. For example, highly saturated inks may be more prone to clogging in pens with fine nibs, while iron gall inks may not be suitable for pens with delicate metal parts.

Consider your writing or artistic goals as well. If you're journaling or taking notes, a reliable and fast-drying ink may be ideal. For artistic projects, you might explore shimmering or pigmented inks for their visual impact. And if archival quality is a priority, pigmented or iron gall inks are excellent choices.

It's also essential to consider the color of the ink. Choose colors that you find visually appealing and that complement the paper you'll be using. Experiment with different ink colors to discover your favorites and to create unique combinations.

2.3 Filling Your Fountain Pen: A Step-by-Step Guide for Different Filling Mechanisms

Filling a fountain pen is a straightforward process, but the exact steps may vary depending on the filling mechanism of your pen. Here's a brief overview of the most common filling mechanisms and how to use them:

- **Cartridge Filling:** Simply insert the cartridge into the barrel of the pen until it clicks into place.
- **Converter Filling:** Dip the nib and feed of the pen into a bottle of ink and turn the converter mechanism (usually a piston or a screw) to draw ink into the converter.
- **Piston Filling:** Turn the piston knob at the end of the pen to expel air from the barrel. Then, dip the nib into ink and turn the knob in the opposite direction to draw ink into the barrel.
- **Vacuum Filling:** Dip the nib into ink and depress the filling mechanism (usually a button or a lever) to create a vacuum that draws ink into the barrel.
- **Eyedropper Filling:** Unscrew the barrel of the pen and use an eyedropper or syringe to fill the barrel with ink.

For each filling mechanism, it's crucial to follow the manufacturer's instructions carefully to avoid leaks or damage to the pen. With a little practice, filling your fountain pen will become second nature.

2.4 The World of Fountain Pen Friendly Paper: What to Look For

The type of paper you choose can significantly impact your fountain pen experience. Not all papers are created equal when it comes to fountain pen ink.

Some papers may bleed or feather, causing the ink to spread and create fuzzy lines.

Fountain pen friendly paper is typically smooth and has a good amount of sizing (a coating that helps prevent ink from bleeding). Look for papers specifically labeled as "fountain pen friendly" or those with high cotton content, as these tend to perform well with fountain pen inks.

Consider the weight of the paper as well. Heavier papers (measured in gsm or grams per square meter) are less prone to bleed-through and offer a more luxurious writing experience.

Experiment with different paper types and brands to find those that complement your inks and writing style. Some popular brands known for their fountain pen friendly papers include Rhodia, Clairefontaine, Tomoe River, and Midori.

2.5 Ink & Paper Pairing: Creating Stunning Combinations

The interplay of ink and paper is where the magic truly happens. By thoughtfully pairing inks and papers, you can create stunning visual and tactile experiences that elevate your writing and artwork.

Consider the color of the ink and how it interacts with the paper's shade and texture. Some inks may appear more vibrant on certain papers, while others may exhibit subtle shading or sheening effects. Experiment with different combinations to discover unique and captivating results.

The texture of the paper can also influence how the ink lays down. Smooth papers tend to produce crisp lines and allow for fine details, while textured papers can add depth and character to your writing.

Don't be afraid to experiment and try unexpected combinations. The world of ink and paper pairing is full of possibilities, waiting to be explored by your creative spirit.

In conclusion, this chapter has taken you on a journey through the fascinating world of ink and paper, the essential partners in your fountain pen adventures. By understanding the different types of inks, their properties, and how to choose the right ones for your needs, you'll be well on your way to creating expressive and captivating writing and artwork. Remember, the possibilities are endless when it comes to ink and paper pairings, so don't hesitate to experiment and discover the combinations that speak to your creative soul.

Chapter 3

Mastering the Basics of Fountain Pen Use: Grip, Angle, Pressure, Cleaning, and More

In this chapter, we delve into the art of using a fountain pen, transforming it from a mere writing instrument into an extension of your hand and an expression of your creativity. We'll guide you through the essential techniques of holding, writing, and maintaining your fountain pen, ensuring a smooth and enjoyable writing experience. From finding the perfect grip and angle to understanding the nuances of pressure and rhythm, you'll learn how to wield your pen with confidence and finesse. We'll also delve into the importance of cleaning and maintaining your pen to ensure its longevity and optimal performance. By the end of this chapter, you'll be well-versed in the fundamental skills that will empower you to create beautiful lettering, calligraphy, and artwork with your fountain pen.

3.1 Holding Your Fountain Pen: Finding the Right Grip & Angle

The way you hold your fountain pen can significantly impact your writing comfort and control. While there's no single "right" way to hold a pen, finding a grip that feels natural and comfortable for you is crucial. Here are some common grip styles:

- **The Tripod Grip:** This is the most widely used grip and involves holding the pen between your thumb, index, and middle fingers. The thumb and index finger gently pinch the pen while the middle finger supports it from below.
- **The Quadrupod Grip:** Similar to the tripod grip, but with the addition of the ring finger resting on the pen for added stability.
- **The Pinch Grip:** This grip involves holding the pen between your thumb and index finger, with the other fingers curled under the palm.

Experiment with different grip styles to find one that feels comfortable and allows you to write for extended periods without strain.

In addition to grip, the angle at which you hold your pen is also important. Aim for a comfortable angle of about 45-60 degrees relative to the paper. This allows for smooth ink flow and prevents the nib from catching or skipping on the paper.

3.2 Writing with a Fountain Pen: Pressure, Speed, & Rhythm

Unlike ballpoint pens, fountain pens require minimal pressure to write. In fact, pressing too hard can damage the nib and hinder ink flow. Let the weight of the pen do the work and focus on maintaining a light and consistent pressure as you write.

The speed at which you write can also affect the line quality. Writing too slowly can cause the ink to pool and create blobs, while writing too quickly can lead to skipping and inconsistent lines. Experiment with different speeds to find a comfortable pace that allows for smooth and even ink flow.

Rhythm is another essential aspect of fountain pen writing. Strive for a consistent rhythm as you form your letters and words. This will create a more natural and flowing writing style.

3.3 Cleaning & Maintaining Your Fountain Pen: Essential Tips & Tricks

Regular cleaning and maintenance are essential for keeping your fountain pen in top condition and ensuring optimal performance. Here are some essential tips and tricks:

- **Flushing:** Flush the pen with cool water every few weeks or whenever you change ink colors. This removes any residual ink and prevents clogging.
- **Soaking:** If your pen is heavily clogged or you're experiencing flow issues, soak the nib and feed in a cup of water for a few hours or overnight.
- **Cleaning the Feed:** Use a soft brush or a cotton swab to gently clean the feed under running water. Be careful not to damage the delicate fins of the feed.
- **Drying:** After cleaning, gently shake the pen to remove excess water and allow it to air dry completely before refilling.

- **Lubrication:** If the piston or filling mechanism feels stiff, apply a small amount of silicone grease to lubricate it.
- **Storage:** Store your pen in a safe and upright position when not in use to prevent leaks or damage.

3.4 Common Fountain Pen Problems & How to Solve Them

Even with proper care, fountain pens can occasionally experience issues. Here are some common problems and how to troubleshoot them:

- **Hard Starts & Skipping:** This can be caused by a clogged feed or nib, insufficient ink flow, or a damaged nib. Try flushing the pen, soaking the nib, or gently adjusting the nib tines.
- **Inconsistent Ink Flow:** This can be caused by a variety of factors, including a clogged feed, a dirty nib, or an air bubble in the ink reservoir. Try flushing the pen, cleaning the nib, or refilling it carefully.
- **Blobbing or Feathering:** This is often caused by using the wrong type of paper or ink. Switch to a fountain pen friendly paper and try a different ink.
- **Leaks:** Leaks can occur due to a damaged or loose filling mechanism, a cracked barrel, or a worn-out O-ring. If you're unable to fix the issue yourself, consult a professional pen repair service.
- **Baby's Bottom:** This refers to a smooth and shiny spot on the nib that can cause skipping

or inconsistent ink flow. It can be caused by excessive pressure or using abrasive paper. Gently polish the nib with micromesh or a polishing cloth to remove the smooth spot.

3.5 Advanced Fountain Pen Techniques: Flex Nibs, Oblique Holders & More

Once you've mastered the basics of fountain pen use, you can start exploring more advanced techniques that can add flair and expression to your writing. Here are a few examples:

- **Flex Nibs:** Flex nibs are designed to create line variation based on pressure. By applying varying pressure, you can create thick and thin lines, adding a dynamic and expressive quality to your writing.
- **Oblique Holders:** Oblique holders are angled pen holders that can help you achieve a more consistent and controlled line angle, especially when writing italic or calligraphy scripts.
- **Flourishing:** Flourishing is the art of adding decorative elements to your writing, such as swirls, loops, and flourishes. It can elevate your calligraphy and lettering to new heights of artistry.
- **Color Mixing:** Experiment with mixing different ink colors to create unique shades and gradients. This can add depth and dimension to your artwork and lettering.
- **Layering:** By layering different ink colors or techniques, you can create complex and visually stunning effects.

As you delve deeper into the world of fountain pens, don't be afraid to experiment and try new techniques. With practice and patience, you'll discover the endless creative possibilities that these versatile writing instruments offer.

In conclusion, this chapter has equipped you with the essential skills and knowledge to master the basics of fountain pen use. By understanding the importance of grip, angle, pressure, rhythm, and maintenance, you'll be well on your way to unlocking the full potential of your fountain pen. Remember, practice makes perfect, so don't hesitate to spend time honing your skills and exploring new techniques. With dedication and passion, you'll soon be creating stunning lettering, calligraphy, and artwork that reflects your unique style and creativity.

Chapter 4

Introduction to Calligraphy: Unveiling the Art of Beautiful Writing

In this chapter, we embark on an enchanting journey into the world of calligraphy, an art form that elevates handwriting into a realm of elegance, beauty, and expression. Calligraphy, derived from the Greek words "kallos" (beauty) and "graphein" (to write), is the art of creating decorative handwriting or lettering with a pen, brush, or other writing instrument. It is a timeless craft that has been practiced for centuries across various cultures, leaving behind a rich legacy of stunning manuscripts, inscriptions, and artistic creations.

We'll begin by unraveling the essence of calligraphy, exploring its diverse styles and scripts. You'll discover the captivating world of Copperplate calligraphy, a classic and timeless script renowned for its elegance and fluidity. We'll then venture into the realm of modern calligraphy, a contemporary take on the art form that embraces a more free-flowing and expressive style. You'll learn about the essential tools and materials needed for calligraphy, from specialized pens and inks to different types of paper. We'll guide you through the fundamental strokes that serve as the building blocks of calligraphy, setting the stage for your journey into this captivating art form.

4.1 What is Calligraphy?: A Brief Overview of Styles & Scripts

Calligraphy is a vast and diverse art form with a myriad of styles and scripts, each with its own unique history, characteristics, and aesthetic appeal. Some of the most prominent calligraphy styles include:

- **Copperplate:** A classic English script characterized by its elegant, flowing lines and contrasting thick and thin strokes.
- **Spencerian:** An American script known for its ornate and flourished style, often used in formal documents and invitations.
- **Italic:** A slanted script with a more casual and informal feel, popular for everyday writing and creative projects.
- **Gothic:** A bold and dramatic script with pointed letterforms, often associated with medieval manuscripts and religious texts.
- **Uncial:** An ancient script with rounded letterforms, known for its readability and simple elegance.
- **Brush Script:** A modern script that mimics the strokes of a brush, offering a more expressive and dynamic style.

Each calligraphy style has its own set of rules and conventions regarding letterforms, stroke order, and spacing. By learning these rules, you can develop your skills and create beautiful and consistent calligraphy.

4.2 Tools & Materials for Calligraphy: Pencils, Pens, Ink, & Paper

To embark on your calligraphy journey, you'll need a few essential tools and materials. These include:

- **Pencils:** Pencils are ideal for practicing calligraphy strokes and letterforms before moving on to ink. Choose a pencil with a soft lead (HB or softer) for smooth and easy writing.
- **Pens:** The most common pens used for calligraphy are dip pens and fountain pens. Dip pens have a nib that is dipped into ink and are known for their flexibility and expressive line variation. Fountain pens have a built-in ink reservoir and offer a more convenient and portable option.
- **Ink:** Calligraphy inks come in various colors and formulations. Choose an ink that is specifically designed for fountain pens or dip pens, as these inks are formulated to flow smoothly and dry quickly.
- **Paper:** Use a smooth, high-quality paper that is specifically designed for calligraphy. This type of paper will prevent ink from feathering or bleeding, ensuring clean and crisp lines.

You may also want to invest in additional tools like a ruler, a T-square, and a lightbox, which can be helpful for creating guidelines and ensuring consistent letterforms and spacing.

4.3 Basic Calligraphy Strokes: The Building Blocks of Letters

Before diving into specific calligraphy styles, it's essential to master the basic strokes that form the foundation of all letterforms. These strokes include:

- **Upstroke:** A light, upward stroke that starts thin and gradually thickens.
- **Downstroke:** A heavier, downward stroke that starts thick and gradually thins.
- **Oval:** A continuous, rounded stroke that forms the basis of many letterforms.
- **Compound Curve:** A combination of an upstroke and a downstroke, creating a flowing and elegant curve.
- **Hairline:** A very thin, delicate stroke used for connecting letters and adding flourishes.

By practicing these basic strokes, you'll develop muscle memory and control, allowing you to create more complex and sophisticated letterforms with ease.

4.4 Copperplate Calligraphy: An Elegant & Timeless Script

Copperplate calligraphy is a classic English script known for its elegant, flowing lines and contrasting thick and thin strokes. It originated in the 17th century and was initially used for engraving copper plates for printing. Over time, it evolved into a popular script for handwriting and calligraphy.

Copperplate script is characterized by its slanted letterforms, flourished capitals, and graceful loops. It requires a flexible nib that can create thick and thin lines with varying pressure.

To learn Copperplate calligraphy, start by practicing the basic strokes and letterforms. Once you're comfortable with the fundamentals, you can move on to more complex letter combinations and words. Pay attention to the spacing between letters and the overall flow of the script to create a harmonious and visually pleasing composition.

4.5 Modern Calligraphy: A Fresh & Expressive Approach

Modern calligraphy is a contemporary take on traditional calligraphy that embraces a more relaxed and expressive style. It often features bouncy letterforms, playful flourishes, and a less rigid adherence to traditional rules.

Modern calligraphy is typically written with a brush pen or a flexible nib, allowing for greater variation in line thickness and style. It's a versatile script that can be used for a variety of purposes, from creating personalized greeting cards and invitations to designing logos and signage.

To learn modern calligraphy, start by experimenting with different brush pens and nibs to find the tools that you enjoy using. Practice basic strokes and letterforms, and don't be afraid to experiment with different styles and variations. Modern calligraphy encourages creativity and individuality, so feel free to express your own unique style through your writing.

In conclusion, this chapter has introduced you to the captivating world of calligraphy, a timeless art form that offers endless opportunities for creative expression. We've explored the diverse styles and scripts of calligraphy, delved into the tools and materials needed to get started, and covered the fundamental strokes that form the building blocks of calligraphy. We've also taken a closer look at Copperplate calligraphy, a classic and elegant script, and modern calligraphy, a fresh and expressive approach. With this foundation in place, you're ready to embark on your own calligraphy journey and discover the joy of creating beautiful and meaningful writing.

Chapter 5

Mastering Letterforms: The Building Blocks of Calligraphy

Embark on an artistic journey of refining your calligraphy skills as we delve into the intricate world of letterforms. In this chapter, we'll dissect the anatomy of both majuscule (uppercase) and minuscule (lowercase) letters, unraveling the secrets of their structure, proportion, and spacing. We'll delve into the graceful art of connecting minuscule letters, ensuring a fluid and harmonious flow in your writing. You'll learn to add finesse and polish to your work by mastering the creation of numbers and punctuation marks. As we progress, we'll explore the enchanting world of flourishes and embellishments, discovering how these decorative elements can elevate your calligraphy to new heights of artistry. Finally, we'll embark on a creative adventure, guiding you through the process of designing your own unique alphabet, allowing you to express your individuality and artistic vision through your lettering.

5.1 Majuscule (Uppercase) Letters: Structure, Proportion, & Spacing

Majuscule letters, also known as uppercase letters, are the grand pillars of your calligraphic compositions. They command attention and set the tone for your writing. Understanding their structure, proportion, and spacing is key to creating visually balanced and aesthetically pleasing calligraphy.

- **Structure:** Each majuscule letter is composed of basic strokes, such as straight lines, curves, and ovals. Mastering these strokes and their combinations is essential for achieving consistent letterforms.
- **Proportion:** Proportion refers to the relationship between the different parts of a letter. For example, the height of the ascender (the part of a letter that extends above the x-height) should be proportional to the height of the x-height (the height of lowercase letters like x or o).
- **Spacing:** Spacing refers to the distance between letters and words. Proper spacing is crucial for readability and visual appeal. Avoid crowding letters too closely together or leaving excessive gaps between them.

By paying close attention to structure, proportion, and spacing, you'll be able to create majuscule letters that are not only beautiful but also legible and well-balanced.

5.2 Minuscule (Lowercase) Letters: Connecting Strokes & Fluidity

Minuscule letters, also known as lowercase letters, are the workhorses of your calligraphic compositions. They form the majority of your writing and are responsible for conveying the flow and rhythm of your script.

- **Connecting Strokes:** In many calligraphy scripts, minuscule letters are connected by flowing strokes that link one letter to the next. Mastering these connecting strokes is essential for creating smooth and elegant writing.
- **Fluidity:** Fluidity refers to the seamless transition between letters and strokes. Aim for a smooth and continuous flow in your writing, avoiding abrupt stops or jerky movements.

Practice writing minuscule letters in groups or words, focusing on the connecting strokes and maintaining a consistent rhythm. As you gain confidence and skill, you'll be able to create beautiful and flowing calligraphic compositions.

5.3 Numbers & Punctuation: Adding Finesse to Your Writing

Numbers and punctuation marks are often overlooked in calligraphy, but they play an important role in conveying information and adding visual interest to your work.

- **Numbers:** When writing numbers in calligraphy, strive for consistency with the style of your letters. Use the same basic strokes and proportions to create numerals that blend seamlessly with your script.
- **Punctuation:** Punctuation marks like commas, periods, and exclamation points should be carefully placed and sized to complement your writing. Pay attention to their placement

relative to the baseline and x-height of your letters.

By mastering the creation of numbers and punctuation marks, you'll be able to add finesse and polish to your calligraphy, making it more professional and visually appealing.

5.4 Flourishes & Embellishments: Enhancing Your Calligraphy

Flourishes and embellishments are decorative elements that can be added to your calligraphy to enhance its beauty and individuality. They can range from simple swirls and loops to more elaborate designs and illustrations.

- **Swirls:** Swirls are graceful, curved lines that can be added to the beginning or end of letters, or used to fill in empty spaces in your composition.
- **Loops:** Loops are circular or elliptical shapes that can be incorporated into letterforms or used as standalone decorative elements.
- **Flourishes:** Flourishes are more elaborate decorations that can add a touch of whimsy or elegance to your writing. They can be inspired by nature, geometric shapes, or abstract designs.

When adding flourishes and embellishments, it's important to maintain balance and harmony with the rest of your calligraphy. Avoid overdoing it, as too many decorations can distract from the beauty of your letterforms.

5.5 Creating Your Own Alphabet: Designing Unique Letterforms

One of the most exciting aspects of calligraphy is the ability to create your own unique alphabet. This allows you to express your individuality and artistic vision through your lettering.

To create your own alphabet, start by experimenting with different letterforms and styles. You can draw inspiration from existing scripts, historical manuscripts, or even everyday objects.

Consider the following factors when designing your letterforms:

- **Style:** Choose a style that resonates with you, whether it's classic, modern, or something entirely unique.
- **Consistency:** Ensure that your letterforms are consistent in terms of style, proportion, and spacing.
- **Readability:** While creativity is encouraged, don't sacrifice legibility for the sake of design.

Creating your own alphabet is a rewarding and creative process that allows you to leave your mark on the world of calligraphy.

In conclusion, this chapter has delved into the intricate world of letterforms, the building blocks of calligraphy. We've explored the structure, proportion, and spacing of majuscule and minuscule letters, the art of connecting strokes and achieving fluidity, the importance of mastering numbers and punctuation, and the creative possibilities of flourishes and embellishments. We've also encouraged you to embark on a journey of self-expression by designing your own unique alphabet. By applying the knowledge and techniques gained in this chapter, you'll be well on your way to creating beautiful, expressive, and personalized calligraphy that reflects your unique artistic vision. Remember, practice is key to mastery, so embrace the journey of learning and experimentation, and let your creativity flow through your pen.

Chapter 6

Beyond Calligraphy: Hand Lettering & Typography: The Playful Fusion of Creativity and Communication

In this chapter, we embark on an exciting exploration beyond the realm of traditional calligraphy, venturing into the vibrant and versatile world of hand lettering and typography. While calligraphy focuses on elegant and stylized handwriting, hand lettering and typography offer a broader spectrum of creative expression, allowing you to craft unique and eye-catching letterforms that convey specific messages and emotions.

We'll delve into the diverse styles of hand lettering, from whimsical and playful to bold and impactful, and discover how to use different tools and techniques to bring your lettering to life. We'll uncover the fundamentals of typography, understanding the nuances of serif, sans serif, and script fonts, and how to choose the right typeface for your project. As we progress, we'll guide you through the exciting process of combining calligraphy and lettering, creating harmonious compositions that showcase the best of both worlds. And finally, we'll step into the digital realm, exploring the tools and techniques for creating stunning digital lettering.

6.1 Hand Lettering Styles: Exploring Diverse & Creative Options

Hand lettering is a playground for creativity, offering a wide range of styles to suit your artistic vision and project goals. Some popular hand lettering styles include:

- **Script Lettering:** Inspired by calligraphy, script lettering features flowing, connected letters that exude elegance and grace.
- **Sans Serif Lettering:** This modern style is characterized by clean, simple letterforms without serifs (the small decorative lines at the ends of strokes).
- **Serif Lettering:** Serif lettering adds a touch of formality and tradition with its small decorative lines at the ends of strokes.
- **Display Lettering:** This bold and eye-catching style is often used for headlines, logos, and signage.
- **Vintage Lettering:** This style evokes a sense of nostalgia with its retro-inspired letterforms and decorative elements.
- **Doodle Lettering:** This playful style incorporates illustrations and doodles into the letterforms, creating whimsical and unique designs.
- **Chalk Lettering:** Inspired by the look of chalk on a chalkboard, this style features textured and imperfect letterforms that exude a rustic charm.

Experimenting with different hand lettering styles allows you to discover your favorites and develop your unique artistic voice. Don't be afraid to mix and match styles, combining elements from different styles to create your own signature look.

6.2 Serif, Sans Serif, & Script Fonts: Understanding the Basics

Typography, the art and technique of arranging type, plays a crucial role in visual communication. Understanding the different types of fonts and their characteristics can help you choose the right typeface for your project.

- **Serif Fonts:** Serif fonts feature small decorative lines at the ends of strokes. They are often associated with tradition, formality, and readability. Popular serif fonts include Times New Roman, Garamond, and Georgia.
- **Sans Serif Fonts:** Sans serif fonts lack the decorative lines of serif fonts. They are known for their clean, modern aesthetic and are often used in digital media and contemporary designs. Popular sans serif fonts include Arial, Helvetica, and Verdana.
- **Script Fonts:** Script fonts mimic handwriting or calligraphy, with flowing, connected letters. They are often used for invitations, greeting cards, and other creative projects. Popular script fonts include Brush Script, Edwardian Script, and Lucida Handwriting.

When choosing a font, consider the tone and message you want to convey. A serif font may be more appropriate for a formal document, while a sans serif font may be a better choice for a modern website.

6.3 Lettering Tools & Techniques: From Markers to Brushes

Hand lettering can be created with a variety of tools, each offering unique effects and textures. Some popular tools include:

- **Markers:** Markers come in a wide range of colors and tip sizes, making them a versatile and convenient tool for lettering.
- **Brush Pens:** Brush pens have flexible tips that mimic the strokes of a brush, allowing for expressive line variation and dynamic lettering.
- **Dip Pens:** Dip pens offer greater control and precision than markers or brush pens, but they require more skill and practice to master.
- **Parallel Pens:** Parallel pens have two parallel plates that create thick and thin lines depending on the angle at which the pen is held.
- **Brushes:** Brushes can be used with watercolor or gouache to create beautiful and expressive lettering.

Experimenting with different tools and techniques is key to discovering your preferences and developing your lettering style.

6.4 Combining Calligraphy & Lettering: Creating Stunning Compositions

Combining calligraphy and lettering opens up a world of creative possibilities, allowing you to create visually striking and expressive compositions. Here are some tips for combining these two art forms:

- **Choose Complementary Styles:** Select calligraphy and lettering styles that complement each other in terms of tone and aesthetic. For example, a classic Copperplate script might pair well with a bold sans serif lettering style.
- **Vary Your Line Weights:** Use different line weights to create contrast and visual interest. For example, you might use a thin, delicate script for calligraphy and a bolder, thicker font for lettering.
- **Play with Color:** Introduce color to your compositions to add vibrancy and personality. Use different ink colors for your calligraphy and lettering, or experiment with watercolor or gouache backgrounds.
- **Consider Composition:** Think about the overall layout and composition of your design. Experiment with different arrangements of your calligraphy and lettering to create a balanced and visually appealing composition.

By thoughtfully combining calligraphy and lettering, you can create unique and expressive artwork that tells a story and captivates the viewer.

6.5 Digital Lettering: Exploring Software & Apps

Digital lettering offers a new dimension of creative expression, allowing you to create stunning lettering designs using software and apps. Popular tools include:

- **Procreate:** This powerful iPad app offers a wide range of brushes, textures, and effects for creating digital lettering.
- **Adobe Illustrator:** This industry-standard vector graphics software is ideal for creating scalable lettering designs that can be used for print and digital media.
- **Affinity Designer:** This affordable alternative to Adobe Illustrator offers similar features and capabilities for creating digital lettering.
- **iPad Lettering Apps:** There are numerous iPad apps specifically designed for lettering, such as Calligraphy Penmanship, iFontMaker, and LetterGlow.

Digital lettering allows for greater flexibility and experimentation than traditional lettering. You can easily undo mistakes, experiment with different colors and styles, and create complex designs that would be difficult to achieve with traditional tools.

In conclusion, this chapter has taken you on an exciting journey beyond the realm of traditional calligraphy, exploring the dynamic and expressive world of hand lettering and typography. We've delved into the diverse styles of hand lettering, uncovered the fundamentals of typography, and explored the tools and techniques for creating both traditional and digital lettering. By embracing the creative possibilities of hand lettering and typography, you can elevate your artistic expression and communicate your message with flair and impact.

Chapter 7

Creative Projects with Fountain Pens: Unleashing the Artistry of Ink

Welcome to the realm where your fountain pen transforms into a wand of creativity! In this chapter, we'll embark on a delightful journey, exploring the myriad ways you can harness the power of your fountain pen to create captivating projects that go beyond simple writing. From journaling and diary entries imbued with elegance to personalized greeting cards and invitations that exude warmth, we'll delve into the diverse applications of fountain pens in everyday life. You'll discover how to elevate your organizational skills with the art of bullet journaling and planning, infusing your schedules with artistic flair. We'll even unleash your inner artist, guiding you through the joys of doodling and drawing with your pen. By the end of this chapter, you'll be brimming with inspiration and equipped with the knowledge to transform ordinary moments into extraordinary works of art with the simple stroke of your fountain pen.

7.1 Journaling & Diary Writing: Adding Elegance to Everyday Notes

In the age of digital distractions, journaling with a fountain pen offers a mindful and intimate way to connect with your thoughts and emotions. The smooth glide of the nib across the paper, the satisfying sound of ink flowing, and the tactile experience of holding a pen in your hand create a sensory symphony that elevates the act of writing.

Your fountain pen becomes a confidant, capturing your musings, reflections, and dreams in elegant script. The unique character of your handwriting, the subtle variations in line thickness, and the nuanced shades of ink all contribute to a personalized journal that is a true reflection of your inner world.

Whether you're jotting down daily reflections, capturing travel memories, or exploring creative ideas, a fountain pen adds a touch of sophistication and soulfulness to your journal entries.

7.2 Greeting Cards & Invitations: Designing Personalized Creations

In a world of mass-produced greetings, handwritten cards and invitations are a cherished expression of thoughtfulness and care. Your fountain pen becomes a tool of personal connection, allowing you to craft unique and heartfelt messages that resonate with the recipient.

With a fountain pen, you can experiment with different lettering styles, from elegant calligraphy to playful hand lettering, to create custom designs that match the occasion and personality of the recipient. Incorporate flourishes, embellishments, and decorative elements to elevate your creations to new heights of artistry.

The tactile quality of a handwritten card or invitation adds a layer of warmth and intimacy that is often lost in digital communication. Your thoughtful gesture will be treasured by the recipient long after the event has passed.

7.3 Bullet Journaling & Planners: Organizing Your Life with Flair

Bullet journaling is a customizable organizational system that combines to-do lists, calendars, and personal notes in a creative and flexible format. Your fountain pen becomes your organizational ally, allowing you to design spreads that are both functional and visually appealing.

Use your fountain pen to create headers, titles, and bullet points that are clear and easy to read. Experiment with different lettering styles and colors to add personality and visual interest to your spreads. Incorporate doodles, drawings, and trackers to personalize your bullet journal and make it a reflection of your unique style.

With a fountain pen in hand, even mundane tasks like scheduling appointments or making to-do lists become enjoyable and creative endeavors.

7.4 Doodling & Drawing: Unleashing Your Inner Artist

Doodling and drawing with a fountain pen is a liberating and playful way to express your creativity. Whether you're sketching intricate patterns, whimsical characters, or abstract designs, your pen becomes a tool of self-discovery and artistic expression.

The varied line widths and expressive capabilities of a fountain pen make it ideal for capturing the nuances of your sketches and drawings. Experiment with different nib sizes, ink colors, and shading techniques to create depth, texture, and visual interest in your artwork.

Don't be afraid to let your imagination run wild. Allow your pen to wander across the page, creating spontaneous lines, shapes, and patterns that reflect your inner world.

7.5 Artistic Projects: Exploring Mixed Media & More

The versatility of fountain pens extends beyond writing and drawing. They can be used in a variety of artistic projects, adding a unique touch to mixed media creations, collages, and even textile art.

Experiment with using your fountain pen in conjunction with watercolors, acrylics, or other art mediums. Create washes of color with diluted ink, or layer ink drawings over painted backgrounds.

Use your fountain pen to add handwritten quotes, poems, or personal messages to your artwork, creating a deeper connection between the viewer and the piece.

The possibilities are endless when you combine the expressive power of a fountain pen with other artistic tools and techniques.

In conclusion, this chapter has unveiled the vast creative potential of fountain pens. By exploring the diverse applications of fountain pens in everyday life, you've discovered how to add elegance to your journaling, personalize your greetings, organize your life with flair, unleash your inner artist through doodling and drawing, and even create stunning mixed media artwork. With your fountain pen as your creative companion, you can transform ordinary moments into extraordinary works of art. Embrace the joy of experimentation, let your imagination soar, and discover the endless possibilities that await you on your artistic journey.

Chapter 8

Inspiration and Resources: Nurturing Your Creative Journey with a Supportive Community

Embark on an enriching exploration of the vibrant and supportive communities that await you on your calligraphy and lettering journey. In this chapter, we'll delve into the wealth of inspiration and resources available online and offline, connecting you with fellow enthusiasts, seasoned experts, and a treasure trove of knowledge. We'll navigate the bustling online calligraphy and lettering communities, where you can find encouragement, feedback, and camaraderie. We'll discover a vast collection of books, courses, and workshops that cater to all skill levels, guiding you through the nuances of this art form. You'll find opportunities to connect with fellow artists at inspiring events and workshops, fostering friendships and collaborations that can fuel your creative fire. And finally, we'll harness the power of social media platforms to showcase your work, connect with a wider audience, and build a thriving creative practice.

8.1 Online Calligraphy & Lettering Communities: Finding Support & Inspiration

The internet has revolutionized the way artists connect and share their work, and the calligraphy and lettering community is no exception. Online platforms offer a wealth of resources, inspiration, and support for artists of all levels.

- **Forums and Groups:** Online forums and groups dedicated to calligraphy and lettering are a haven for enthusiasts to connect, share their work, ask questions, and exchange tips and tricks. Platforms like Reddit, Facebook Groups, and specialized forums provide a space for open discussions and collaborative learning.
- **Online Courses and Tutorials:** Numerous websites and platforms offer online courses and tutorials on calligraphy and lettering, ranging from beginner to advanced levels. These resources often include video demonstrations, practice exercises, and feedback from instructors, making them a valuable resource for learning new techniques and honing your skills.
- **Blogs and Websites:** Calligraphy and lettering blogs and websites are a treasure trove of inspiration, tutorials, and information. Many artists share their creative process, tips, and insights on their blogs, offering valuable learning opportunities for aspiring calligraphers and letterers.

- **Social Media:** Platforms like Instagram, Pinterest, and YouTube are bustling with calligraphy and lettering communities, showcasing stunning artwork, tutorials, and behind-the-scenes glimpses into artists' studios. Engaging with these communities can provide a wealth of inspiration and motivation.

Connecting with online communities can be a transformative experience for artists. The encouragement, feedback, and camaraderie you find online can fuel your creativity and propel your artistic journey forward.

8.2 Books & Courses: Learning from Experts & Masters

Books and courses are invaluable resources for deepening your understanding of calligraphy and lettering. They offer structured learning experiences, expert guidance, and access to the knowledge and wisdom of seasoned professionals.

- **Calligraphy Books:** A vast array of calligraphy books cater to all skill levels and interests. From comprehensive guides on specific scripts to books focusing on lettering styles, techniques, and creative projects, there's a book out there to suit every learner.
- **Online Courses:** Online courses provide a flexible and accessible way to learn calligraphy and lettering at your own pace. They often offer structured lessons, video demonstrations,

practice exercises, and opportunities for feedback from instructors.

- **Workshops & Classes:** In-person workshops and classes offer a more immersive learning experience. You'll have the opportunity to interact with instructors and fellow students, receive hands-on guidance, and practice your skills in a supportive environment.

Investing in books and courses can significantly accelerate your learning and help you develop your skills more effectively. Whether you prefer the solitary learning experience of books or the interactive environment of workshops and classes, there are resources available to suit your learning style.

8.3 Workshops & Events: Connecting with Fellow Enthusiasts

Calligraphy and lettering workshops and events are not only opportunities to learn and refine your skills, but also to connect with fellow enthusiasts and build a supportive community. These gatherings create a space for artists to share their passion, exchange ideas, and foster friendships that can last a lifetime.

- **Calligraphy Workshops:** Calligraphy workshops often focus on specific scripts or techniques, allowing you to delve deeper into a particular area of interest. You'll receive expert instruction, practice your skills, and gain valuable feedback from instructors and peers.

- **Lettering Retreats:** Lettering retreats offer a more immersive experience, combining workshops, social activities, and opportunities for relaxation and reflection. They provide a space for artists to connect on a deeper level, share their creative journeys, and find inspiration in a supportive environment.
- **Conferences and Conventions:** Calligraphy and lettering conferences and conventions bring together artists from around the world to showcase their work, learn from experts, and network with industry professionals. These events are a hub of creativity and inspiration.

Attending workshops and events can be a transformative experience, providing you with new skills, insights, and friendships that can enrich your artistic journey.

8.4 Social Media Platforms: Sharing Your Work & Gaining Exposure

Social media platforms have become powerful tools for artists to showcase their work, connect with a wider audience, and build a following. Platforms like Instagram, Pinterest, and Facebook offer a visually engaging way to share your calligraphy and lettering creations with the world.

By consistently posting high-quality images of your work, engaging with other artists, and using relevant hashtags, you can increase your visibility and attract followers who appreciate your style. Social media can also be a platform for collaboration, networking, and even finding paid opportunities.

Remember to be authentic and genuine in your online interactions. Share your creative process, your inspirations, and your struggles. By connecting with others on a personal level, you can build a supportive community and gain valuable exposure for your work.

8.5 Building Your Creative Practice: Tips & Tricks for Staying Motivated

Developing a consistent creative practice is essential for growth and progress in calligraphy and lettering. Here are some tips for staying motivated and inspired:

- **Set Goals:** Establish clear goals for your creative practice, whether it's mastering a new script, completing a specific project, or participating in a workshop.
- **Schedule Time:** Dedicate regular time in your schedule for calligraphy and lettering practice. Even short bursts of practice can make a significant difference over time.
- **Find Inspiration:** Look for inspiration in the world around you. Visit museums, art galleries, or libraries. Follow other artists on social media, or browse calligraphy and lettering books and magazines.
- **Join a Community:** Connect with other artists online or in person. Share your work, ask for

feedback, and participate in challenges and collaborations.

- **Experiment:** Don't be afraid to try new techniques, styles, and tools. Embrace experimentation as a way to learn and grow as an artist.

Remember, building a creative practice takes time, dedication, and perseverance. Celebrate your successes, learn from your mistakes, and never lose sight of your passion for calligraphy and lettering.

In conclusion, this chapter has opened the doors to a world of inspiration and resources that can nurture your creative journey in calligraphy and lettering. By engaging with online communities, exploring books and courses, attending workshops and events, leveraging social media platforms, and building a consistent creative practice, you'll be well on your way to becoming a skilled and passionate artist. Embrace the journey, connect with others, and let your creativity flow freely. The world of calligraphy and lettering is yours to explore and conquer!

Chapter 9

The Art of Ink Mixing & Color Theory: Elevating Your Calligraphy and Lettering with Vibrant Hues

Embark on a colorful journey into the captivating world of ink mixing and color theory, where your artistic expression knows no bounds. In this chapter, we'll delve into the fundamentals of color theory, understanding the interplay of hues, saturation, and value to create harmonious and visually stunning compositions. You'll learn the secrets of creating custom ink colors, transforming your palette into a personalized spectrum of shades and tones. We'll explore the unique properties of different inks, from shimmering metallics to deep, rich hues, and how to leverage their characteristics to elevate your calligraphy and lettering. You'll discover how to choose the perfect colors for your projects, creating cohesive palettes that evoke specific moods and emotions. And finally, we'll guide you in using color strategically to enhance your artwork, adding depth, dimension, and a touch of magic to your creations.

9.1 Understanding Color Theory: The Basics of Hue, Saturation, & Value

Color theory is the foundation of visual art, providing a framework for understanding how colors interact and how to use them effectively. The three fundamental elements of color theory are:

- **Hue:** Hue refers to the pure color itself, such as red, blue, or yellow. It's the name we give to a particular wavelength of light.
- **Saturation:** Saturation refers to the intensity or vibrancy of a color. A highly saturated color is bright and pure, while a low-saturated color is dull and muted.
- **Value:** Value refers to the lightness or darkness of a color. A high-value color is light, while a low-value color is dark.

By understanding the interplay of hue, saturation, and value, you can create harmonious color schemes that evoke specific emotions and enhance the visual appeal of your artwork.

9.2 Creating Custom Ink Colors: Tips & Techniques for Mixing

One of the most exciting aspects of working with fountain pen inks is the ability to create your own custom colors. This allows you to personalize your palette and achieve unique shades that perfectly match your creative vision. Here are some tips and techniques for mixing ink colors:

- **Start with a Base Color:** Choose a base color as your starting point. This will be the dominant hue in your custom color.
- **Add Modifiers:** Gradually add small amounts of other ink colors to modify the hue, saturation, and value of your base color. Experiment with different combinations to achieve the desired effect.
- **Keep Track of Your Ratios:** Record the amounts of each ink you use so you can recreate your custom color in the future.
- **Use a Color Mixing Chart:** A color mixing chart can be a helpful tool for visualizing how different colors interact and for predicting the outcome of your mixes.
- **Practice and Experiment:** Don't be afraid to experiment and try different combinations. The more you practice, the more confident you'll become in your ink mixing skills.

Creating custom ink colors is a rewarding and creative process that allows you to express your individuality and expand your artistic palette.

9.3 Exploring Different Ink Properties: Sheening, Shading, & Shimmering

Fountain pen inks offer a variety of unique properties that can add depth and dimension to your calligraphy and lettering. Some of these properties include:

- **Sheening:** Sheening refers to the iridescent sheen that some inks exhibit when dry. This effect is created by the interplay of light and the ink's chemical composition.

- **Shading:** Shading refers to the variation in color intensity within a single stroke. This effect is most noticeable with broader nibs and can create a sense of depth and texture.
- **Shimmering:** Shimmering inks contain metallic particles that add a touch of sparkle and shine to your writing. They can be used to create festive and eye-catching designs.

Experimenting with inks that exhibit these properties can add an extra layer of visual interest to your artwork.

9.4 Choosing Colors for Calligraphy & Lettering: Creating Harmonious Palettes

Choosing the right colors for your calligraphy and lettering projects is essential for creating harmonious and visually appealing compositions. Here are some tips for creating effective color palettes:

- **Consider the Mood:** Think about the mood or emotion you want to evoke with your artwork. Warm colors like red, orange, and yellow can create a sense of energy and excitement, while cool colors like blue, green, and purple can evoke calmness and serenity.
- **Use a Color Wheel:** A color wheel is a helpful tool for visualizing color relationships and creating harmonious palettes. Complementary colors (opposite each other on the color wheel) create high contrast, while analogous colors

(next to each other on the color wheel) create a more harmonious and subtle effect.

- **Limit Your Palette:** Don't overload your artwork with too many colors. Choose a few key colors that work well together and use them consistently throughout your composition.
- **Consider the Background:** The color of your paper or background will influence how your ink colors appear. Choose ink colors that contrast well with the background to ensure readability and visual impact.

By carefully choosing your colors, you can create calligraphy and lettering that is not only beautiful but also emotionally resonant and visually effective.

9.5 Using Color to Enhance Your Artwork: Creating Mood & Atmosphere

Color is a powerful tool that can be used to enhance your artwork and create specific moods and atmospheres. Here are some tips for using color strategically in your calligraphy and lettering:

- **Create Depth:** Use light and dark colors to create a sense of depth and dimension in your artwork. Lighter colors tend to recede, while darker colors appear to advance.
- **Emphasize Focal Points:** Use bright or contrasting colors to draw attention to specific elements of your artwork, such as a particular letter or word.

- **Evoke Emotions:** Different colors evoke different emotions. Use warm colors to create a sense of warmth and energy, or cool colors to evoke calmness and serenity.
- **Tell a Story:** Use color to tell a story or convey a message. For example, you might use a warm color palette to represent a summer day or a cool color palette to depict a winter scene.

By thoughtfully using color, you can transform your calligraphy and lettering into powerful visual expressions that resonate with viewers on an emotional level.

In conclusion, this chapter has explored the vibrant world of ink mixing and color theory, empowering you to elevate your calligraphy and lettering with captivating hues. By understanding the fundamentals of color theory, mastering ink mixing techniques, exploring different ink properties, and choosing colors strategically, you can create artwork that is both visually stunning and emotionally resonant. Remember, color is a powerful tool in your artistic arsenal, so don't hesitate to experiment and explore the endless possibilities it offers.

Chapter 10

Fountain Pens & Fine Art: A Symphony of Ink and Imagination

In this chapter, we embark on an enchanting journey where the fountain pen transcends its role as a writing instrument and becomes a versatile tool for artistic expression. We'll delve into the captivating world of fountain pen art, exploring its unique techniques, expressive possibilities, and boundless potential. From the delicate washes of watercolor painting to the intricate details of sketching and drawing, you'll discover how your fountain pen can be a powerful instrument for capturing the world around you and expressing your innermost emotions. We'll explore the enchanting fusion of ink and watercolor, creating mesmerizing mixed media artworks that blend the fluidity of ink with the vibrant hues of water-based pigments. As we journey further, we'll venture into the realm of fountain pen illustration, where storytelling and visual narratives come to life through the delicate strokes of your pen. And finally, we'll embrace the freedom of experimentation, encouraging you to explore diverse art styles and techniques, from abstract to impressionistic, to create truly unique and personal works of art.

10.1 Watercolor Painting with Fountain Pen Ink: A Unique Approach

Watercolor painting with fountain pen ink offers a refreshing and unconventional approach to this beloved medium. The water-soluble nature of fountain pen ink allows for a unique interplay of line and wash, creating delicate and ethereal effects that are difficult to achieve with traditional watercolor paints.

Using a fountain pen with a brush nib or a flexible nib, you can create both fine lines and broad washes of color. Experiment with different ink colors and dilution ratios to achieve a wide range of tonal variations. Apply washes of color first, and then use your pen to add details, outlines, and textures. You can also create interesting effects by drawing with your pen on wet watercolor washes, allowing the ink to bleed and diffuse, creating soft and organic shapes.

Watercolor painting with fountain pen ink is a versatile technique that can be used for a variety of subjects, from landscapes and portraits to still life and abstract compositions. Embrace the fluidity and spontaneity of ink and water to create unique and expressive artworks.

10.2 Sketching & Drawing with Fountain Pens: Capturing Details & Textures

Fountain pens are not just for writing; they can also be powerful tools for sketching and drawing. The variety of nib sizes and ink colors available allows for a wide range of expressive possibilities, from capturing fine details to creating bold, gestural lines.

Using a fountain pen with a fine nib, you can create intricate line drawings that capture the nuances of your subject matter. Experiment with cross-hatching, stippling, and other shading techniques to add depth and dimension to your sketches.

For a more expressive approach, try using a broader nib or a brush pen. These tools allow you to create bold lines, dramatic strokes, and textured washes of color. You can also experiment with different ink colors to add vibrancy and personality to your drawings.

Fountain pen sketching and drawing is a versatile technique that can be used for a variety of purposes, from capturing everyday observations to creating detailed illustrations.

10.3 Combining Ink & Watercolor: Creating Stunning Mixed Media Art

The fusion of ink and watercolor creates a mesmerizing interplay of line and wash, resulting in stunning mixed media artworks that are both delicate and expressive.

Start by creating a watercolor wash on your paper. Use your fountain pen to add details, outlines, and textures. The ink will interact with the wet watercolor, creating interesting bleeds, blooms, and diffusions. You can also use your pen to draw on top of dry watercolor washes, adding a layer of detail and definition.

Experiment with different ink and watercolor combinations to discover unique and unexpected results. For example, try using a waterproof ink to create crisp lines that resist the watercolor washes, or use a water-soluble ink to create soft, blended effects.

Mixed media art with ink and watercolor offers endless possibilities for creative expression. It's a technique that allows you to combine the best of both worlds, creating artworks that are both visually stunning and emotionally evocative.

10.4 Fountain Pen Illustration: Exploring Storytelling & Visual Expression

Fountain pen illustration is a powerful tool for storytelling and visual expression. With a few simple lines and strokes, you can bring characters to life, depict scenes from your imagination, or capture the essence of a moment in time.

Start by sketching out your ideas on paper. Use your fountain pen to add details, shading, and textures. Experiment with different line weights and styles to create depth and visual interest.

Consider the composition of your illustration, thinking about how the different elements of your drawing will work together to tell a story or convey a message. Use color strategically to enhance your illustration and create a specific mood or atmosphere.

Fountain pen illustration is a versatile medium that can be used for a variety of purposes, from creating children's books and graphic novels to illustrating personal journals and travelogues.

10.5 Experimenting with Different Art Styles: Abstract, Impressionistic, & More

Don't limit yourself to traditional drawing and painting techniques. Embrace the freedom of experimentation and explore different art styles with your fountain pen.

- **Abstract:** Create abstract compositions by focusing on lines, shapes, and colors rather than realistic representation. Let your intuition guide you as you experiment with different techniques and approaches.
- **Impressionistic:** Capture the fleeting impressions of light and color by using loose brushstrokes and a limited color palette. Focus on capturing the essence of your subject matter rather than its precise details.
- **Minimalist:** Embrace the power of simplicity by using a few essential lines and shapes to create impactful and evocative artwork.
- **Expressionistic:** Express your emotions and feelings through bold colors, distorted forms, and exaggerated lines.

By experimenting with different art styles, you can expand your creative horizons and discover new ways of expressing yourself through your fountain pen.

In conclusion, this chapter has opened the doors to a world of artistic expression with fountain pens. By exploring techniques like watercolor painting, sketching, drawing, mixed media art, and illustration, you've discovered the versatility and potential of this humble writing instrument. Embrace the joy of experimentation, let your creativity flow freely, and don't be afraid to break the rules and create your own unique artistic style. Remember, the only limit is your imagination!

Chapter 11

Advanced Calligraphy Techniques: Elevate Your Artistry with Flourishes, Scripts, and Flourishing

Welcome to the realm of advanced calligraphy techniques, where your artistic expression soars to new heights of elegance and sophistication. In this chapter, we'll embark on a journey of mastery, delving into the intricate world of flourishing, embellishments, and specialized scripts that will transform your calligraphy into breathtaking works of art. You'll learn to embellish your letterforms with graceful flourishes, adding decorative elements that enhance their beauty and individuality. We'll explore the intricacies of classic scripts like Spencerian and Gothic, unearthing their historical significance and unique characteristics. You'll master the versatile italic hand, a script that seamlessly blends elegance and informality. And finally, we'll venture into the realm of offhand flourishing, where spontaneous and free-flowing designs add a touch of whimsy and personality to your calligraphy.

11.1 Flourishing & Embellishments: Adding Decorative Touches to Your Writing

Flourishing and embellishments are the jewels that adorn the crown of calligraphy. These decorative elements can transform simple letterforms into breathtaking works of art, adding personality, flair, and a touch of magic to your writing.

- **Basic Flourishes:** Start by mastering basic flourishes, such as simple loops, swirls, and curves. These fundamental elements can be added to the beginning or end of letters, or used to fill in empty spaces in your composition.
- **Advanced Flourishes:** As you gain confidence, explore more complex flourishes, such as intricate loops, spirals, and floral designs. These embellishments can be inspired by nature, geometric shapes, or abstract concepts.
- **Incorporating Flourishes:** Integrate flourishes seamlessly into your calligraphy by ensuring they complement the letterforms and enhance the overall flow and rhythm of your writing. Avoid overdoing it, as too many flourishes can overwhelm the composition.
- **Personalizing Your Style:** Develop your unique flourishing style by experimenting with different shapes, sizes, and combinations of decorative elements. Your flourishes can become a signature element of your calligraphy, reflecting your individuality and artistic vision.

By mastering the art of flourishing and embellishments, you'll be able to elevate your calligraphy to new heights of artistry and create truly unique and personalized works of art.

11.2 Spencerian Script: A Classic & Ornate Style of Calligraphy

Spencerian script is a classic American script renowned for its ornate and flourished style. It was developed in the mid-19th century by Platt Rogers Spencer and quickly became the dominant handwriting style in the United States. Spencerian script was widely used in formal documents, business correspondence, and even everyday writing.

- **Characteristics:** Spencerian script is characterized by its elegant, flowing lines, delicate hairlines, and dramatic shades (thick downstrokes). The letterforms are often adorned with flourishes, loops, and other decorative elements.
- **Tools & Materials:** Spencerian script is traditionally written with a flexible pointed nib and black ink. However, modern calligraphers often use oblique pen holders and a variety of inks to create their own unique interpretations of this classic script.
- **Learning Spencerian:** Mastering Spencerian script requires patience, practice, and attention to detail. Start by learning the basic strokes and letterforms, and gradually progress to more complex words and phrases. Pay close

attention to the angle of your pen, the pressure you apply, and the rhythm of your strokes.

Spencerian script is a beautiful and challenging script that offers endless opportunities for artistic expression. By mastering this classic style, you'll be able to create stunning calligraphy that evokes a sense of history and elegance.

11.3 Gothic Script: Exploring Medieval & Renaissance Lettering

Gothic script, also known as blackletter, is a bold and dramatic script with pointed letterforms that originated in medieval Europe. It was widely used for religious texts, manuscripts, and official documents, and its influence can still be seen in modern typography and design.

- **Characteristics:** Gothic script is characterized by its angular letterforms, heavy downstrokes, and elaborate flourishes. The script is often written in black ink on parchment or vellum, creating a striking and dramatic effect.
- **Variations:** There are many different variations of Gothic script, including Textura, Rotunda, Schwabacher, and Fraktur. Each variation has its own unique characteristics and historical context.
- **Learning Gothic Script:** Mastering Gothic script requires patience, practice, and an understanding of its historical context. Start by learning the basic strokes and letterforms of a specific Gothic variation, and gradually

progress to more complex words and phrases. Pay close attention to the angles, proportions, and spacing of your letters.

Gothic script is a powerful and expressive script that can be used to create stunning calligraphic compositions. By exploring the different variations of Gothic script, you can add a touch of history and drama to your lettering.

11.4 Italic Calligraphy: A Versatile & Expressive Hand

Italic calligraphy is a slanted script known for its versatility and expressive qualities. It originated in Italy during the Renaissance and quickly gained popularity throughout Europe. Italic script is characterized by its flowing lines, graceful curves, and dynamic contrast between thick and thin strokes.

- **Characteristics:** Italic script is a relatively easy script to learn, making it a popular choice for beginners. However, it also offers ample opportunity for advanced calligraphers to explore its expressive potential.
- **Variations:** There are many different variations of italic script, including Chancery cursive, Copperplate italic, and modern italic. Each variation has its unique characteristics and can be used for a variety of purposes, from formal documents to personal correspondence.
- **Learning Italic Calligraphy:** To learn italic calligraphy, start by practicing the basic strokes and letterforms. Pay attention to the

angle of your pen, the pressure you apply, and the spacing between letters. Once you've mastered the fundamentals, you can experiment with different variations and develop your own unique style.

Italic calligraphy is a versatile and expressive script that can be used for a variety of purposes, from everyday writing to artistic creations. By mastering this classic hand, you'll be able to add a touch of elegance and personality to your writing.

11.5 Offhand Flourishing: Mastering Free-flowing & Spontaneous Designs

Offhand flourishing is a dynamic and expressive form of calligraphy that involves creating spontaneous and free-flowing designs. Unlike traditional flourishing, which follows specific rules and patterns, offhand flourishing is more intuitive and improvisational.

- **Characteristics:** Offhand flourishing is characterized by its organic, flowing lines, playful curves, and unexpected twists and turns. It's a style that encourages experimentation and individuality.
- **Tools & Materials:** Offhand flourishing can be created with a variety of tools, including fountain pens, brush pens, and even markers. The choice of tool will depend on your personal preference and the desired effect.
- **Learning Offhand Flourishing:** The best way to learn offhand flourishing is to simply start experimenting and playing with different

strokes and patterns. Don't be afraid to make mistakes and let your creativity flow. As you practice, you'll develop your own unique style and learn to create stunning and original designs.

Offhand flourishing is a fun and rewarding way to add personality and flair to your calligraphy. It's a style that encourages you to let go of perfectionism and embrace the joy of spontaneous creation.

In conclusion, this chapter has explored the world of advanced calligraphy techniques, from flourishing and embellishments to specialized scripts like Spencerian, Gothic, and italic. We've also delved into the expressive world of offhand flourishing, where creativity and spontaneity reign supreme. By mastering these techniques, you'll be able to elevate your calligraphy to new heights of artistry and create unique and personalized works of art that reflect your individual style and vision. Embrace the challenge, explore the possibilities, and let your creativity flow freely. The world of calligraphy is yours to conquer!

Chapter 12

Building a Business with Your Skills: From Passion to Profit in Calligraphy and Lettering

Embark on an entrepreneurial journey as we delve into the exciting realm of transforming your calligraphy and lettering passion into a thriving business. In this chapter, we'll guide you through the essential steps of establishing and growing a successful creative enterprise. You'll learn how to determine fair and competitive prices for your work, considering factors like skill level, time investment, and market demand. We'll explore effective marketing strategies to reach potential clients and customers, showcasing your unique talents and offerings. You'll discover the importance of building a compelling portfolio that highlights your best work and attracts potential clients. We'll delve into the intricacies of working with clients, from understanding their needs to delivering exceptional results that exceed expectations. And finally, we'll explore the fulfilling path of teaching and conducting workshops, allowing you to share your knowledge and passion with others while expanding your business.

12.1 Pricing Your Work: Determining Fair & Competitive Rates

One of the most crucial aspects of building a successful calligraphy and lettering business is setting appropriate prices for your work. It's a delicate balance between valuing your time, skills, and experience, while also remaining competitive in the market.

- **Cost of Materials:** Calculate the cost of materials used in each project, including paper, ink, pens, and any other supplies.
- **Time Investment:** Track the time you spend on each project, from initial consultation to final delivery. This includes research, design, execution, and communication with the client.
- **Skill Level:** Consider your level of expertise and experience in calligraphy and lettering. More experienced artists can generally command higher rates.
- **Market Research:** Research the rates charged by other calligraphers and letterers in your area or niche. This will give you a benchmark for setting your own prices.
- **Value-Based Pricing:** Consider the value your work brings to the client. If your work helps a client achieve a specific goal or outcome, you can charge a premium for that value.

It's also important to be transparent and upfront about your pricing with clients. Clearly communicate your rates and any additional fees, such as rush fees or revisions, to avoid misunderstandings later on.

12.2 Marketing Your Skills: Reaching Potential Clients & Customers

Marketing is essential for getting your work seen by potential clients and customers. It's about showcasing your unique talents and offerings in a way that resonates with your target audience.

- **Website or Online Portfolio:** Create a professional website or online portfolio to showcase your work. Include high-quality images, client testimonials, and clear contact information.
- **Social Media:** Utilize social media platforms like Instagram, Pinterest, and Facebook to share your work, engage with potential clients, and build a community of followers.
- **Networking:** Attend industry events, workshops, and conferences to connect with potential clients and other professionals in your field.
- **Collaborations:** Partner with other businesses or artists to cross-promote each other's work and reach a wider audience.
- **Referrals:** Encourage satisfied clients to refer you to their friends and colleagues. Word-of-mouth marketing can be incredibly powerful.

Remember, marketing is an ongoing process. Consistently promote your work, engage with your audience, and stay up-to-date with the latest trends and technologies to ensure your business stays relevant and competitive.

12.3 Building Your Portfolio: Showcasing Your Best Work

Your portfolio is your calling card, a visual representation of your skills, style, and experience. It's essential to curate a portfolio that showcases your best work and highlights your versatility as an artist.

- **Diversity:** Include a variety of projects that demonstrate your range of skills and styles. This might include calligraphy samples, lettering designs, logos, illustrations, and other creative projects.
- **Quality:** Only include your highest quality work in your portfolio. Ensure that images are well-lit, sharp, and accurately represent your skills.
- **Relevance:** Tailor your portfolio to your target audience. If you specialize in wedding calligraphy, for example, make sure your portfolio features a variety of wedding-related projects.
- **Presentation:** Present your portfolio in a professional and visually appealing format. Consider creating a physical portfolio book or a digital portfolio website.

Your portfolio is a living document that should be updated regularly as you create new work and refine your skills.

12.4 Working with Clients: Creating Custom Calligraphy & Lettering Projects

Working with clients can be a rewarding and challenging experience. It requires strong communication skills, creative problem-solving, and a commitment to delivering exceptional results.

- **Understanding Client Needs:** Take the time to understand your client's vision, goals, and expectations for the project. Ask questions, clarify details, and ensure you're both on the same page.
- **Proposal & Contract:** Provide a detailed proposal outlining the scope of work, timeline, deliverables, and payment terms. Once the proposal is approved, create a contract that both parties sign to protect everyone's interests.
- **Design & Execution:** Use your artistic skills and expertise to create custom calligraphy and lettering designs that meet or exceed the client's expectations.
- **Communication & Feedback:** Maintain open communication with your client throughout the project. Provide regular updates, seek feedback, and be responsive to any questions or concerns.
- **Delivery & Payment:** Deliver the final product on time and in the agreed-upon format. Invoice the client promptly and follow up to ensure timely payment.

Building strong client relationships is key to repeat business and referrals. Strive to provide exceptional service, deliver high-quality work, and exceed your client's expectations.

12.5 Teaching & Workshops: Sharing Your Knowledge & Passion

Teaching calligraphy and lettering workshops can be a fulfilling way to share your knowledge and passion with others, while also generating additional income for your business.

- **Developing Workshop Curriculum:** Design a workshop curriculum that is engaging, informative, and tailored to your target audience. Consider offering beginner, intermediate, and advanced workshops to cater to different skill levels.
- **Marketing Your Workshops:** Promote your workshops through your website, social media, email list, and local community events.
- **Creating a Welcoming Environment:** Create a comfortable and supportive learning environment where students feel encouraged to explore their creativity.
- **Delivering Engaging Instruction:** Use a variety of teaching methods, such as demonstrations, hands-on exercises, and group discussions, to keep students engaged and motivated.
- **Providing Individualized Feedback:** Offer constructive feedback to each student, helping

them identify areas for improvement and achieve their calligraphy and lettering goals.

Teaching workshops allows you to connect with other artists, inspire creativity, and build a community around your shared passion for calligraphy and lettering.

In conclusion, this chapter has equipped you with the essential tools and knowledge to transform your calligraphy and lettering passion into a thriving business. By mastering the art of pricing, marketing, portfolio building, client management, and teaching, you can create a successful and fulfilling career that allows you to share your artistic talents with the world. Remember, building a business takes time, dedication, and perseverance. Embrace the challenges, learn from your experiences, and never lose sight of your passion for creating beautiful and meaningful lettering. The world is your canvas, and your fountain pen is your brush. Let your creativity flow and build a business that reflects your unique artistic vision.

Printed in Great Britain
by Amazon

50618181R00046